Travel Adventures

Yosemite

Perimeter and Area

Dona Herweck Rice

Consultants

Michele Ogden, Ed.D
Principal
Irvine Unified School District

Colleen Pollitt, M.A.Ed.
Math Support Teacher
Howard County Public Schools

Publishing Credits

Rachelle Cracchiolo, M.S.Ed., *Publisher*
Conni Medina, M.A.Ed., *Managing Editor*
Dona Herweck Rice, *Series Developer*
Emily R. Smith, M.A.Ed., *Series Developer*
Diana Kenney, M.A.Ed., NBCT, *Content Director*
Stacy Monsman, M.A., *Editor*
Kevin Panter, *Graphic Designer*

Image Credits: p.7 Library of Congress [LC-USZ62-120024]; p.8 Stock Montage/Getty Images; p.9 (left and right) Courtesy of the Yosemite National Park Archives, Museum, and Library; p.10 age fotostock/Alamy Stock Photo; p.11 Keystone/Underwood Archives/Getty Images; p.12 MPI/Getty Images; p.14 (left) Barbara Alper/Getty Images, (right) Library of Congress [LC-USZC4-5573]; all other images from iStock and/or Shutterstock.

Library of Congress Cataloging-in-Publication Data

Names: Rice, Dona, author.
Title: Travel adventures : Yosemite / Dona Herweck Rice.
Other titles: Yosemite
Description: Huntington Beach, CA : Teacher Created Materials, [2018] |
  Includes index. | Audience: Grades 4-6. | Description based on print
  version record and CIP data provided by publisher; resource not viewed.
Identifiers: LCCN 2017012139 (print) | LCCN 2017019031 (ebook) | ISBN
  9781480759428 (eBook) | ISBN 9781425855604 (pbk.)
Subjects: LCSH: Yosemite National Park (Calif.)--Juvenile literature.
Classification: LCC F868.Y6 (ebook) | LCC F868.Y6 R53 2018 (print) | DDC
  979.4/47--dc23
LC record available at https://lccn.loc.gov/2017012139

Teacher Created Materials

5301 Oceanus Drive
Huntington Beach, CA 92649-1030
http://www.tcmpub.com

ISBN 978-1-4258-5560-4

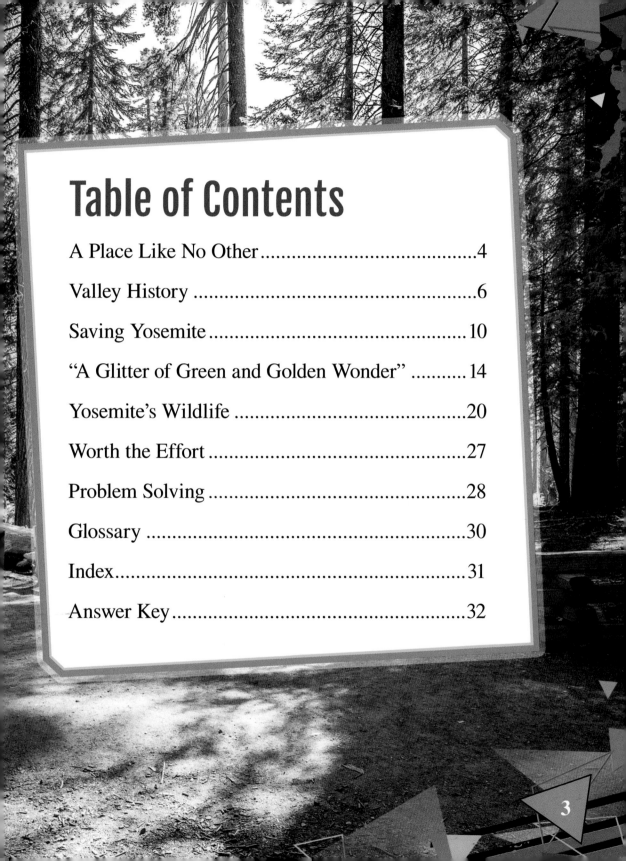

Table of Contents

A Place Like No Other

There's green as far as the eye can see. But only in spring and summer, of course. In winter, shades of white, blue, and purple streak the mountains and valleys. Year round, there is a lake so clear you can see reflections of mountains and sky. Standing at the water's edge, it's like looking into an upside-down world. There are tree-lined trails that give hikers shady comfort on even the hottest summer days. Towering cliffs, plunging waterfalls, and ancient domes seem like the stuff of movies rather than the real world. Bears, elk, and deer roam wild. Bats dot the evening sky with flapping wings and piercing cries. Mosquitoes and stinging bugs, dragonflies and butterflies, and all manner of flying creatures are everywhere. *Everywhere.*

This is the majestic world of Yosemite. It has a natural beauty that is not found in many places. Millions of tourists agree it is one of the most breathtaking places in the world!

Valley History

Long before people came to Yosemite Valley, the rocky mountain cliffs and snaking waterways were already much like we know them today. Plant life flourished. Animals settled in this thriving place. It was a rich environment.

People first came to the area about 8,000 years ago. They hunted for food with spears and gathered seeds and other plants to eat. **Archaeologists** (ahr-kee-AWL-uh-jists) have found some traces of their lives. Fossils and tools they used have taught us much of what we know about them. Stories have also been passed down through the ages. But, no one knows exactly when the stories began.

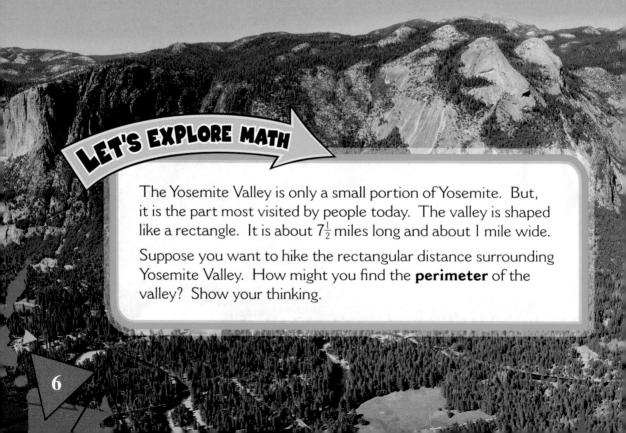

LET'S EXPLORE MATH

The Yosemite Valley is only a small portion of Yosemite. But, it is the part most visited by people today. The valley is shaped like a rectangle. It is about $7\frac{1}{2}$ miles long and about 1 mile wide.

Suppose you want to hike the rectangular distance surrounding Yosemite Valley. How might you find the **perimeter** of the valley? Show your thinking.

At some point, these people called the place they lived *Ahwahnee*. That was their word for "**gaping** mouth." A gaping mouth is what the wide valley looked like to them. Many think it looks that way still.

About 4,000 years ago, American Indians moved into the valley. These people were called Miwok (MEE-wok). The name simply means "people." That is what they called themselves. By the late 1700s, the valley was filled with Miwok. They thrived in this environment. It offered everything they needed to live well.

A Miwok man spearfishes in a creek.

Gold Rush

Life in Yosemite changed greatly in 1849. That year marked the start of California's Gold Rush. Thousands of people from all over the country swooped into the area. They wanted to get rich quickly. In their frenzy for gold, miners often pushed the Miwok off their land and out of their homes. Some Miwok were killed. Some died of starvation because their resources were taken. Others fought back, trying to preserve their way of life.

Miners search for gold in California in 1849.

Remember that Yosemite Valley is about $7\frac{1}{2}$ miles long and about 1 mile wide. Now, consider its **area**.

Imagine that a huge storm passed over Yosemite Valley, and the ground is all covered in snow. Use the area model to find the number of square miles of snow covering the valley.

1 sq. mi.

In time, most Miwok who stayed adapted to western **culture**. They began to dress like westerners. They began to eat western types of food. They took jobs in service to the newcomers. Some served as guides for those who had just arrived. They showed the new residents how to live in Yosemite, even though their own way of life was falling away.

In time, the number of Miwok dwindled. Today, fewer than 1,000 Miwok live in the area. They have worked to maintain and restore traditions of their culture.

A Miwok tribe meets for a morning council in Yosemite Valley in 1872.

Miwok woman and her baby

9

Saving Yosemite

Two men named Hutchings and Ayres went to Yosemite in 1855. They wrote and drew about the area. Then, they shared what they saw with others. Many people wanted to see it for themselves. The Wawona Hotel was built so that visitors would have a place to stay. A tunnel was carved through a giant sequoia called the Wawona Tree so they could drive right through it. The tree became a huge tourist attraction.

Soon, more businesses were built. People tramped all over Yosemite. They used the land and built for **commercial** gain. They built homes. They took pieces as souvenirs. People **exploited** the beauties of Yosemite for their own gain. They didn't take action to preserve the land for the future.

A group of **conservationists** grew worried. They wanted to protect Yosemite. These people made sure that the president of the United States knew about the problem. Abraham Lincoln joined their cause in 1864. He placed part of the land in **public trust**. This was the first time the government set up such protections for public land. It was an act that would mark the start of the national park movement.

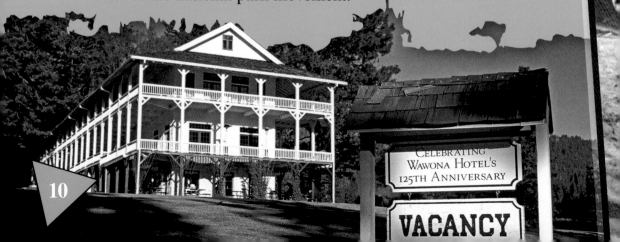

CELEBRATING
WAWONA HOTEL'S
125TH ANNIVERSARY

VACANCY

The rectangular opening to the tunnel in the Wawona Tree was 7 feet across and 9 feet tall before the tree toppled in 1969.

1. Draw a model of the tunnel opening. Label the dimensions.

2. Use the model to find the perimeter and area of the tunnel opening.

Visitors drive through the Wawona Tree in 1910.

President Theodore Roosevelt and John Muir visit Glacier Point in Yosemite, California.

Becoming a National Park

Yellowstone became the first national park in 1872. It was placed under the care of the U.S. government. People would still be able to enjoy the park but in ways that wouldn't harm it.

Naturalist John Muir wanted the same for Yosemite. Sheep grazing had taken its toll on the land. Railroad tracks laid nearby brought many tourists. Despite the public trust, the land was overrun and overused. Yosemite was in danger.

Muir spent years getting people to work with him to protect Yosemite. He wrote often about its wonders. He thought that such wild places were key to the health of the earth. He wrote, "All that the sun shines on is beautiful, so long as it is wild."

In 1890, the U.S. Congress set aside part of the area as a national park. But Muir thought more needed to be done. In 1903, he asked President Theodore Roosevelt to camp with him in Yosemite. Roosevelt was a fan of the outdoors and agreed to come. He was awed by what he saw. Muir convinced him to protect all of Yosemite. In 1906, he declared all of it a national park.

UNITED STATES
DEPARTMENT OF THE INTERIOR
NATIONAL PARK SERVICE

YOSEMITE NATIONAL PARK

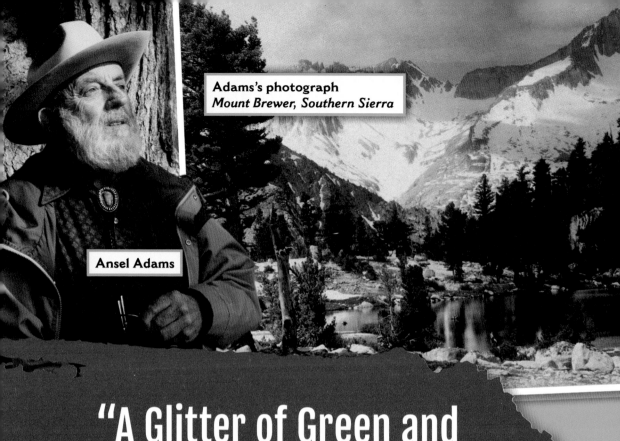

Adams's photograph
Mount Brewer, Southern Sierra

Ansel Adams

"A Glitter of Green and Golden Wonder"

Ansel Adams was a famous photographer who took many photos of the park. He thought it was one of the most striking places on Earth and even lived there for a while. He called Yosemite "a glitter of green and golden wonder"—a colorful caption for his black-and-white photos of the park.

The park is found in the Sierra Nevada Mountains. It is 1,169 square miles (3,028 square kilometers). Its landscape was first formed 10 million years ago. The uplift of Earth's crust shaped the land. Then, about one million years ago, glaciers carved the mountain rock.

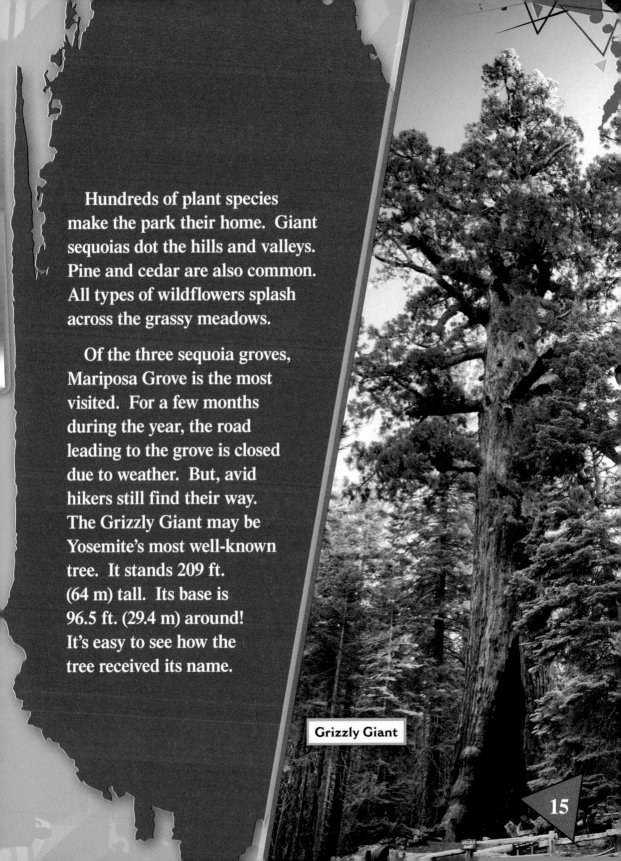

Hundreds of plant species make the park their home. Giant sequoias dot the hills and valleys. Pine and cedar are also common. All types of wildflowers splash across the grassy meadows.

Of the three sequoia groves, Mariposa Grove is the most visited. For a few months during the year, the road leading to the grove is closed due to weather. But, avid hikers still find their way. The Grizzly Giant may be Yosemite's most well-known tree. It stands 209 ft. (64 m) tall. Its base is 96.5 ft. (29.4 m) around! It's easy to see how the tree received its name.

Grizzly Giant

Bridalveil Fall

Besides the Grizzly Giant, another well-known site in Yosemite is Bridalveil Fall. The waterfall looks just like its name sounds. Water billows like the soft flowing fabric of a bride's veil. Its drop is 620 ft. (189 m) from top to bottom. With enough wind, the water can blow sideways, making it seem even more like a veil.

Water at the fall flows all year long, although it is strongest in the spring. It is fed by Bridalveil Creek. The creek, in turn, is fed by Ostrander Lake, about 10 mi. (16 km) away.

Bridalveil Fall

LET'S EXPLORE MATH

Bridalveil Fall is about 20 meters across and about 200 meters tall. Imagine that the surface of the waterfall freezes and is made of squares of ice measuring 1 meter on each side.

How many square meters of ice make up the surface of the frozen waterfall? Show your strategy for finding the solution.

Yosemite Falls

Yosemite Falls

Compared to Yosemite Falls, Bridalveil may seem like only a trickle. Yosemite Falls is the tallest of the park's more than 20 falls. It is 2,425 ft. (739 m) tall. That is nearly half a mile. It is taller than almost all of the world's skyscrapers!

Yosemite Falls is really made of three waterfalls. Each fall cascades into another. As with most falls in the park, water flows freely in the spring but can dry up by late summer. Autumn rain and winter snow return the falls to flowing. Yosemite Creek feeds the falls, which then flow into the Merced River.

Half Dome

Half Dome is one of the most famous domes in the world. Rising 5,000 ft. (1,524 m) over Yosemite Valley, its rocky face glints in the sun. People come from all around the world to hike the tough trail. Just when they think they've reached their goal, they have to climb the last 400 ft. (122 m) with only two metal cables to help them. Looking down may make hikers nervous as they **ascend**. But, they are safe if they are careful. Most injuries are just blisters and twisted ankles. After completing the 10-to-12-hour round-trip, hikers return with a great story to tell.

Hikers climb Half Dome.

Half Dome

El Capitan

El Capitan is the world's largest granite **monolith**. It is 13,114 ft. (3,997 m) tall. That's about $2\frac{1}{2}$ mi. (4 km)! Its height makes it a popular spot to climb. Climbers usually take between two and three days to reach the **summit**, or top. More advanced climbers can reach it in 24 hours. Known as El Cap, it is also popular for BASE jumps. BASE stands for *building*, *antenna*, *span*, and *earth*. These are fixed structures from which jumpers take their leaps. Many people have climbed or jumped from El Cap and have lived to tell the tale. But, that's not true for everyone.

El Capitan

Yosemite's Wildlife

John Muir was a naturalist who seemed to have the heart of a poet. Speaking of Yosemite's wildlife, he wrote, "How many hearts with warm red blood in them are beating under cover of the woods, and how many teeth and eyes are shining!" He went on, "A multitude of animal people, intimately related to us, but of whose lives we know almost nothing, are as busy about their own affairs as we are about ours."

Muir studied the animals of Yosemite almost like he studied the land. It was easy to do! Animals are everywhere you turn. Visitors can see them day and night. They come in all shapes and sizes. Mule deer, bobcats, and black bears live there in large numbers. Bats fill the night sky. Spotted owls and falcons take to the air as well. Foxes and **skinks** skitter along the ground. Rivers and lakes are filled with fish. Muir certainly was right; Yosemite is alive with its "animal people"!

peregrine falcon

bobcat

skink

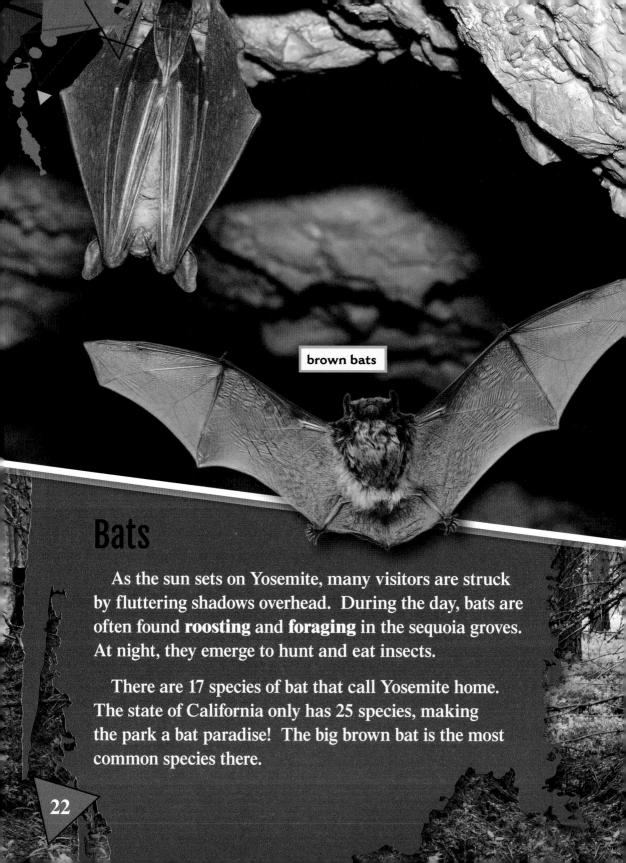

brown bats

Bats

As the sun sets on Yosemite, many visitors are struck by fluttering shadows overhead. During the day, bats are often found **roosting** and **foraging** in the sequoia groves. At night, they emerge to hunt and eat insects.

There are 17 species of bat that call Yosemite home. The state of California only has 25 species, making the park a bat paradise! The big brown bat is the most common species there.

Black Bear

Bears can also be found in the park. However, only about 300 to 500 black bears live there. It's not unheard of to see a bear, but it's not a common sight either. Bears generally don't like to walk among people. But, campers must be careful where they leave food. Hungry bears are known to raid tents. Bears can even smell food inside locked cars. It doesn't take much for them to break in!

When bears can't find human food, they eat mainly berries, grasses, and acorns. They may eat meat, but it's not their typical diet. It's important for campers to help ensure that bears eat what nature provides. Human food is not healthy for them!

LET'S EXPLORE MATH

Imagine that rangers measure the rectangular floor of a black bear's den in Yosemite. They discover that the den is 6 feet long and has a perimeter of 20 feet. How can they find the width of the den floor? Show your strategy.

den

black bear

Sierra Nevada bighorn sheep

Sierra Nevada Bighorn Sheep

Sierra Nevada bighorn sheep once roamed Yosemite in huge numbers. Adept at climbing rocky hillsides, they thrived in the park's high ranges. But disease and hunting wiped out the bighorn population in the park's first 25 years.

In time, conservationists were able to protect the species. They relocated sheep outside of Yosemite but still within the Sierra Nevada mountains. Later, they returned a few herds to the park. After nearly a century-long absence, the bighorn may return to the numbers they once had.

Mule Deer

Mule deer are the most easily spotted mammal in Yosemite. They are named for their big ears that look like a mule's. These deer communicate with their ears. They point them forward when they sense danger. They flatten them to their heads when angry.

Mule deer eat shrubs and herbs. But they are a main food source for many predators, too. Visitors to Yosemite often try to feed mule deer. They are fooled by the deers' gentle looks. But the deer are wild animals. Many people are kicked or butted. Good thing, too. Human food can make the deer sick or dependent on humans.

mule deer

Worth the Effort

"Between every two pine trees there is a door leading to a new way of life." John Muir wrote these words in the margin of his notebook. He was speaking of Yosemite.

Muir found the beauty of Yosemite's landscape and wildlife inspiring. Countless visitors to Yosemite agree. Although visits are governed and the park is protected, people still come to Yosemite in droves. They hike its mountains. They explore its valley. They wade in its rivers and bike its trails. They camp in the forest or look out at the wild terrain from the window of a lodge. For just a little while, they make Yosemite their home, too.

"It is good for everybody," Muir also wrote about Yosemite. "None can escape its charms. Its natural beauty cleans and warms like a fire, and you will be willing to stay forever in one place like a tree."

Many people wish they could. They'd dig in their roots, sprout their leaves, and stand with the Grizzly Giant watching over the beautiful landscape known as Yosemite.

# Problem Solving

Yosemite National Park is a popular place to vacation. Imagine you have been asked to build cabins for tourists. You must design four different cabins. Each cabin, no matter the size, should have a rectangle-shaped living area and a perimeter of 60 feet.

1. What is the length and width of the living areas of each of your four cabin designs? Sketch each design on graph paper, and label the dimensions.

2. How many square feet make up each cabin design? Explain your thinking.

3. What pattern do you notice in your strategies for finding the perimeter of each of your designs?

4. What pattern do you notice in your strategies for finding the area of each of your designs?

Glossary

archaeologists—scientists who study humans of the past and their activities through the items they leave behind

area—the amount of space covered by square units inside a two-dimensional shape

ascend—to go up

commercial—having to do with earning money

conservationists—people who work to protect and preserve the natural world and its resources

culture—the belief, practices, customs, language, art, and music of a group of people living at the same time in the same place

exploited—used someone or something in a way that helped you unfairly

foraging—looking for food

gaping—spread wide open

monolith—a tall and narrow stone formation

naturalist—person who studies and explores nature

perimeter—the distance around the outside of a shape

public trust—system by which lands are held for use by all

roosting—making a home in a nest

skinks—type of lizard

summit—the top, or highest point, of a mountain

Index

Answer Key

Let's Explore Math

page 7:

17 miles; $7\frac{1}{2} + 1 + 7\frac{1}{2} + 1 = 17$;
Answers will vary, but may
include drawing a sketch of the
rectangle, labeling the dimensions,
and adding all four measurements.

page 8:

$7\frac{1}{2}$ square miles; count the number
of squares

page 11:

1. Model should be labeled as
    a 7 foot × 9 foot rectangle

2. Perimeter = 32 ft.;
    Area = 63 sq. ft.

page 16:

4,000 square meters; Strategies
will vary, but may include drawing
a sketch and multiplying the length
and width.

page 23:

4 ft.; Answers will vary. Possible
strategy: 6 + 6 = 12;
20 − 12 = 8; 8 ÷ 2 = 4

Problem Solving

1. Answers may vary.
    Possible answers:
    10 ft. × 20 ft., 12 ft. × 18 ft.,
    15 ft. × 15 ft., and
    16 ft. × 14 ft.

2. Answers may vary.
    Possible answers:
    10 ft. × 20 ft. = 200 sq. ft.;
    12 ft. × 18 ft. = 216 sq. ft.;
    15 ft. × 15 ft. = 225 sq. ft.;
    16 ft. × 14 ft. = 224 sq. ft.

3. Answers will vary, but may
    include that the perimeter
    can be found by multiplying
    the length by 2, multiplying
    the width by 2, and adding
    the products; or, by adding
    the length and width and
    multiplying the sum by 2;
    or, by adding all sides.

4. Answers will vary, but may
    include that the area can be
    found by multiplying the
    length and width.